DARK WATER AT NIGHT

OWEN KNIGHT

LEFTHANDPRESS
NEW ORLEANS, LOUISIANA USA

ISBN: 978-0692826225

United States • United Kingdom • Europe • Australia • India

PREFACE

On a bright morning. There is the smell of red clover. Then, somewhere, a cardinal's call. Beyond the clover, a broken wooden chair, Wonderland blue. Then under the clouds, the fields and woodlands. This was the start. At the end there will be the smell of red clover; the broken wooden chair, Wonderland Blue. Then, somewhere, a cardinal's call.

For Anne,
with love and gratitude for her assistance
in the preparation of this manuscript,
and a thank you to Jo Bounds for his design and layout.

CONTENTS

YULETIDE GREETING

This Yule we come with singing.
Carols and games and charms we are bringing.
Flow water. Flowing, flowing, flowing.
Blow wind. Blowing, blowing.
We come to greet the Yule,
Holly, and Ivy, fool King and King Fool.
Rise sun. Rising, rising, rising.
Run deer. Running, running.

SWEET BAY WREATHS WITH CANDLES

Sweet Bay wreaths with candles,
And holly on the walls.
It's Christmas Eve.
The great piano burst with Christmas song.
Stockings are hung with hope.
A letter to old Santa Claus is going up
in smoke.
Supper is by candle light.
Stars look down on a land pure white.
Over all is a mystic light.

Elfin Christmas Song

Silver bells began to play
And a star shown in the heavens,
Lit the night as bright as day.

Golden balls hung on the pine.
From its limbs dripped silver tinsel.
Raised were cups of ruby wine.
Tromping through the fallen snow,
Cheerful mummers sang their carols
As they wandered to and fro.

Elves and goblins blessed the Yule.
Trolls and boogiemen and brownies
Cheered the king, the mighty fool.

Leaving halls of flickering light,
Santa Claus, his gray beard wagging,
Rode his sleigh into the night.

GREENSLEEVES AND THE GREEN GIANT

It was one yuletide long ago,
To Camelot the Jolly Green Giant did go.
Past the angry porter who stood at the door,
The Giant, on his horse, tromped over the floor.

Greensleeves was his desire.
Her sparkling green eyes set his heart on fire.
Grensleeves was his delight.
To honour his love he would gladly fight.
Greensleeves, his one true joy,
'Twas all for the love of Greensleeves.

"Why came he to Camelot?" King Arthur would know.
"Why to give and take gifts, one blow for one blow."
Then all the Knights' laughter lay under a pall.
The spirit of giving had fled from the hall.

Greensleeves was his desire.
Her sparkling green eyes set his heart on fire.
Grensleeves was his delight.
To honour his love he would gladly fight.
Greensleeves, his one true joy.
'Twas all for the love of Greensleeves.

Some there were, paled to behold the Giant's size,

11

It seemed none desired to receive such a prize.
Wouldn't gifts not so strange serve to honour the Yule?
To accept such gifts be a game for a fool.

Greensleeves was his desire.
Her sparkling green eyes set his heart on fire.
Grensleeves was his delight.
To honour his love he would gladly fight.
Greensleeves, his one true joy,
'Twas all for the love of Greensleeves.

Said Gawain, "I grant your outrageous boon.
I shall give you your blow and that quite soon.
You shall not insult this company more."
He struck and a green head rolled on the floor.

Greensleeves was his desire.
Her sparkling green eyes set his heart on fire.
Grensleeves was his delight.
To honour his love he would gladly fight.
Greensleeves, his one true joy,
'Twas all for the love of Greensleeves.

There sat Sir Kay, his moith open wide
To behold the Green Giant still seated astride.
Sir Ulfin looked down with shock and surprise
To see the head smiling and winking its eyes.

Greensleeves was his desire.
Her sparkling green eyes set his heart on fire.
Grensleeves was his delight.
To honour his love he would gladly fight.

Greensleeves, his one true joy,
'Twas all for the love of Greensleeves.

Then spoke the green head and that, loud and clear
That the King and all of the knights should hear.
"For my gift, may I thank you. That scratch I shall wear.
Get yours at my castle, the Yule of next year."

Greensleeves was his desire.
Her sparkling green eyes set his heart on fire.
Grensleeves was his delight.
To honour his love he would gladly fight.
Greensleeves, his one true joy,
'Twas all for the love of Greensleeves.

The Giant shook the reigns of his horse once more.
Rode to his head which had rolled down the floor.
As the guest was by none invited to stay,
He picked up his head and rode on his way.

Greensleeves was his desire.
Her sparkling green eyes set his heart on fire.
Grensleeves was his delight.
To honour his love he would gladly fight.
Greensleeves, his one true joy,
'Twas all for the love of Greensleeves.

THE JOY OF GROUNDHOG DAY

The joy of Groundhog Day is come
With stick and rock and ox horned mask.
Now let the elders join the hum;
Let some, the sacred objects bring.
Step forward to your annual task,
And when the pipe begins to sing,
Begin the ritual, join the thing.
What's the ritual? What's the thing?
And why the stick and rock and mask?
I think it strange that you should ask.

Eboracum Has Come Again

He comes back, his bow of yew,
His red arrow will fly true,
His ax defeats the lords of frost.
They will retreat for they have lost.

Salute the spring. Her flowers will fill
Every valley, every hill
Shall burn with light lit from the spark
From the bow of Mighty York.

In the woods, the fires of green
On winning warriors will be seen.
With Angus Og, with Washington,
Lord York has come and he has won.

Salute the spring. Her flowers will fill
Every valley, every hill
Shall burn with light lit from the spark
From the bow of Mighty York.

GOLDEN DAFFODILS

I saw the Golden Daffodils
I heard their laughter echo round the hills

One day some clowns cam calling,
But long they wouldn't stay.
With dainty lace and painted face,
They left and went far away.
Yet now their bell like laughter,
Their little scraps of song
Like merry ghosts keep coming back
To cheer me the whole summer long.
Yet still the bell like laughter,
Each little frill of song,
Scrap by scrap keeps coming back
To cheer me the whole summer long.

MOONLIGHT SNOW IN MID JULY

The trees shake their shadows in the
warm July night.
The river breezes blow.
The moon comes out.
The world is bathed in magic white.
All is still a still cool white.
It is deep in the yards,
On roofs and trees,
Drift in the winding road,
Moonlight Snow.
It was a mid summer night.
In stillness were poplar leaves bright,
The roof of the summer house light,
In the boxwood garden.
Before my eyes
Were falling great splotches of white,
Falling faster
and it was snowing.

REDBIRDS IN THE CLOUDS

Pretty bird Pretty bird
Ta Ta Ta
Eek Eek
Whit Whit Whit
Pretty Bird
Red Birds in the clouds
Eek Eek
Whit Whit
Whiffle Whish
Whish Steek Steek
Urble why
Eek Eek
Whit Whit Whit

CLOSE TO NATURE'S PINK DREAMS

On Young's Spring Hill
The new grass,
A cool sunlight,
Springs up in airs transparency.
Huge, pink dreams float.
About a dead tree,
The blue sky falls and folds,
A sheer silk sheet about a post.
Dream clouds fade
To cool, clear, white far clouds.
Evernear,
The dead tree flutters
Like a ghost.

BLUE DRUID MARCH

A hazy mist that suddenly appears
And silently
Steals away
And with the mist
A noiseless column of blue
Moves
with easy flowing motion

Grey blue jacket
Grey blue cap
Beard and face with blue tint
Dignified step and solemn face
March in the early morn.
They pass as if on some urgent mission.
A little gust of wind and the mist lifts.
A little ripple of blue
As a rock thrown into a silent pool
And the Druids vanish.

O THE NIGHT IS ALL ABOUT IN EASY DANCES

O The Night Is All About in Easy Dances.
O the moon has wandered with the plantain stone.
O the blaching light has sucked the darkness out of the
shadows.
O the uneasy rocking has snuffed the carol out of the
golden girl.
O the easy night is passing, she is gone.
O the moon has sucked the comfort out of shadows.
O the sky is in the ragweed's fiberous stem.
O the night is slanted. Night is everywhere upon the
golden girl.
O the lilies wrap the bosom of a friend.

O The Night is All About in Easy Dances.
O the moon has sat upon the plantain stone.
O here with blanching moonlight,
O the shadows swaying in uneasy rocking,
The easy night is passing, she is gone.

THE BATTLE OF THE BIRDS

Huge black birds were in the air,
They fought the golden dragons there
As, far below, King Arthur knights
Clashed with the knights of Lot and Lear.
Then they did stop the battle fierce.
They drank out of their flagons
While, high above them in the air,
The black bird fought the dragons.
Sir Echel and Sir Kay drove up
A pale and dark horse riding.
Arthur's spokesmen stout were they.
With the enemy they'd been biding.
Oh will they give up the hostages?
I hear the dragons sighing.
Will they give hostages? They will not?
Then let commence the fighting.
Dance, pale maidens.
Now it seems you'll have the companions shortly.
The tall young knights here soon will fall.
Then some, be bald and portly.
Prince Flamdwyn and King Fewdor Flam
Pressed on fiercely, but in vain;
As did King Uriens, to their right,
His helm and white beard shining bright.
Sir Neal and Nantess, in the press,

Contended hotly for the field
In equal fight. Here each must fall,
For surely neither one would yield.
Then came envoys riding up:
Sir Bredbeddle and Sir Bors.
Hard they rode to Arthur's flag,
Each on his sweating horse.
Then they did stop the battle fierce.
They drank out of their flagons
While, high above the battle field,
The black birds fought the dragons.
Oh, will they give up hostages?
I hear the black birds crying.
They will give none. They will fight on.
Then, we will all be dying.
A host lay bleeding on the plain.
Sir Echel and Sir Rhun were slain.
Then the best Knight in the land
Was to fall by Flamdwyn's hand
While in pursuit of Fewdor Flam:
The flower of knighthood, Sir Owein.
The many naked maidens there;
Each one graceful, each one fair;
Shall wait a youthful, moonlit host,
Shall dance as lightly as a ghost.

THE BATTLE AT DUGLASS RIVER

No graying hair. Face forever fair.
Strike and fall
into the dark waters
Of the Duglass River,
Forever young.
No graying hair. Face forever fair.
Strike and fall
 into the dark waters
Of the Duglass River
Which flows outward to the sea,
Forever young.

THE DARK SHIP

Sir Bedevere returned from the margin of the Lake, past
Where Sir Lucan Lay fading into death, to where Lay his
Mortally wounded sire, King Arthur.

"Sire," He said. "I beheld a marvelous thing. I flung
Escalibur, as you commanded, far out into the Lake; but,
Before it touched the water's surface, a white hand rose
Up, grabbed it by the hilt, three times the sword it waved;
Then, hand and sword together vanished beneath the
water." "It is well".

Said the king, "But your dawdeling has wasted precious
time; so, make haste, assist me to yonder brook. I go to
Avallon."

Sir Bedvedere looked up. he beheld an even greater
   marvel
Than he had witnessed at the Lake. Up the brook, which
Flowed close at hand, drifted a coal black barque. A
Gentle breeze filled a single black sail. And in the barque
Stood three black robed queens, black robed and black
Hooded, and these, the Queen of Northgalis, The Queen
of Out Islands and Morgan the Fay. Sir Bedivere carried
his king to a place which the dark ship approached. The
three queens reached down, gently lifted the king from Sir

Bedivere, lay him down between them. The ship sailed
on, sailed up the brook, "Sire, what I am to do," called
Sir Bedivere after the departing ship, "of all the fellowship,
There's none Left but me?"

There was a cry in the heart of the sky. Whether, spirit
Or bird, Bedivere knew not, but more answer there was
none.

The ship sailed on, sailed up the brook, into the distance
And was seen no more.

THE WHITE SAIL

In the still cool sunlight of the morning
The tops of the Lindens sway.
There is a white sail
Out on the blue water of the bay.
The wind blows on this high hill
Sighs loud through boughs of the great trees.
It isn't there that white sail, nor any blue water.
There is only this   stiff breeze.

GOING TO LEICESTER

The sea nymphs are singing
A dim isle is seen
A transparent silver
A sparkle green

Golden clouds hang o'r the Land of Manannan,
Which hovers just over the horizon's blue rim.
With the freshness of morning, at first light of day,
The sea nymphs are singing, away come away
Come away gently as the dew from the lawn,

Come to the deep isle
In the rose and gold dawn.
Now as the sunbeams
Bequeath their first ray,

The golden ghost island is floating away.
But still the sweet voice of a sea nymph is heard,
Mixed with voice of a clear throated bird,
Come away gently as dew from the lawn,
Come to the deep isle in the rose and gold dawn.

The sea nymphs are singing,
Away come away.
The sea nymphs are singing,
Away come away.

FLOATING ISLAND OF GLASS

We will keep you from harm,
In life, the rocks were sharp and cold.
We will keep you from harm.
Dread not a rose's faint alarm.

We will guard you from harm.
Shadows fall. Dark waters creep.
We will guard you from harm.
Falling shades are naught but sleep.

Warrior, Come out of the world of suffering mankind
Into the darkness of no time
That is not dark, but lit with ghostly light
That burns with a cold brightness.
You will not mind, for you will not be cold
In this place where we dance and pass
The flasks of fiery wine. As you weave
Among our turning bodies pale as moonlit
Streams, all the memories of the world
You knew, as gentle ripples on a starlit pool,
Will be faint, fleeting dreams.

We will keep you from harm,
In life, the rocks were sharp and cold.
We will keep you from harm.
Dread not a rose's faint alarm.

We will guard you from harm
Shadows fall. Dark waters creep.
We will guard you from harm.
Falling shades are naught but sleep.

Warrior,
The castle's turning on its silent isle
Where, in a shower of bright teardrops,
Clear spirits stay. Here, where neither is there
Night nor day, past battles fade,
Our bare bright bodies will not change.
Warrior, come away.

We will keep you from harm,
In life, the rocks were sharp and cold
We will keep you from harm.
Dread not a rose's faint alarm.

We will guard you from harm
Shadows fall. Dark waters creep.
We will guard you from harm.
Falling shades are naught but sleep.

The Towers of Avallon

Dreams,
A land of dreams
Silvery bells of apple blooms
And streams
Moonlit streams.
Dreams.
A land of dreams
Dreams.
This is a land of dreams.
Silvery boughs of apple trees
Garland crystal streams.
Here Rhiannon's singing birds
Unloose their morphic powers
While bubbling brooks sing endlessly
Through ferny banks of flowers.
And into myrtle bowers,
Drop by drop each liquid note
Falls where pearly petals float
Above the drowsing flowers.
This is a land of dreams.
Over paths that lead away
From Avallon's pale towers,
Breezes touch the leafy limbs.
Here slip the endless hours.
Caressed by moonlight beams,

Softly, sweetly bell notes weep
To the things that dream and sleep.
This is a land of dreams.
Silvery bells of apple blooms
And steams
Moonlit streams.
Dreams.
A land of dreams.
Dreams.

This is a land of dreams.
Silvery boughs of apple trees
Garland crystal streams.
Here Rhiannon's singing birds
Unloose their morphic powers
While bubbling brooks sing endlessly
Through ferny banks of flowers.
And into myrtle bowers,
Drop by drop each liquid note
Falls where pearly petals float
Above the drowsing flowers.
This is a land of dreams.
Over paths that lead away
From Avallon's pale towers,
Breezes touch the leafy limbs.
Here slip the endless hours.
Caressed by moonlit beams;
Softly, sweetly bell notes weep
To the things that dream and sleep.
This is a land of dreams.

Dreams,
A land of dreams,

Silvery bells of apple blooms
And steams,
Moonlit streams.
Dreams, A land of dreams,
Dreams.

Going Dancing

High away over the ocean
It is a pale mist weaves a silver haze.
Floating shivering screens
Hang over a green garden
And a starlit day.
Through the endless blue sky
Silently float the billowy clouds
Over a crystal tower.
On a tower they sail like snow
On a field of night.
Under the clouds' fiery white,
On a tower so clear so darkly blue,
Flower pale girls to silent music
Glide and whirl on a silver floor.
It is I that will float in a crystal tower
And the white haired maidens hour on hour,
To a music too pure for ear to hear,
Too clear, too clear, too dark and true,
Forever to glide and weave,
Forever to bend and whirl,
Slender bodies of the water girls,
Fragil sails on sleepy summer seas,
Forever glide.
On an island over the sea
Forever glide.

Away I'll be sailing away
To an island over the sea
Where the water maids under the apple trees
Dance and sway in the bright air,
Dance and sway,,, all in an endless day,
Under the silver bough
Of the pale apple bloom,
Where by the little waves
Flow the bright bodies bare
While the petals fall,,, in the water blue,
In the clear air.

QUEEN OF THE FALLING STARS

Towers with lovely jewels of light
Hover over a vast darkness.
There, amid the gloom of
Jagged black shadows,
Pale slim harpers
Touch their strings
Where Gware Golden Hair
Is held by tall blue chains
That reach up and up
Into the sky.
The towers revolve.
Echoey falls of song
Cascade through glittery dark
And maidens hand out,
One by one,
Goblets sparkling, crystal clear.
Then, Lady Silverwheel is there;
Her eyes, the midnight air,
Are framed by floating, flowing
Death pale hair.
Her slender fingers shimmer like
Starlit ice.

ANGELS OF DARK WATER AND NIGHT

Kha Kaaaa –
Three pale angels – flowing robes –
Angels singing pass –
Through the still waters –
Past the bent hair nerve –
Shining through the dark water –
Kha Kaaaa –
They pass –
Through the cool waters –
Past the gold stinging hair nerve –
Always coming, always echoing, reverberating –
Kha kaaaa –
They pass –
Transparent white angels –
Flowing robes –
Singing pass the flashing nerve –
Ever empty, hollow singing –
Ever singing –
Kha kaaa –
They pass –
Angels of dark water,
Angels of night, –
Singing past the hairpin nerve
Always singing –
Always singing –
Always singing –
Kha kaaaaaaaaaaa

Towers Among the Stars

At last, there is
The castle of the Northern Crown
In luminous dark.
A haunting loveliness at the
Back of a dream quest –
The castle is turning
Turning high in dark northern air.
Turrets swinging through
The thin, clear air
Amid the glittery stars.
Seen vaguely there,
The near transparent outline of a
Sad eyed, slender girl.
In naught but a starry crown –
In one hand,
Lightly held,
A ball of twine.

GLEM WARRIORS

Flickering campfires guttering low,
High above in the tall, dark trees,
The lonesome winds forever blow.
Sleep, for with the coming dawn
You'll have a long long way to go.
You'll have a long long way to roam
Unless below the fields of Glem
You'll in silent, dreamless sleep
Lie far from home,
So far from home.

FORGOTTEN CITY

A high arched bridge.
A winding stairway leads up
To a ridge.
Monuments, carven, loom up
Through the trees.
Between buildings tumble waterfalls,
Wind stairs.
Bridges over bridges
Arch on high.
Falling water echoes from the building walls.
The wind howls ghostly answer through the halls.
Tall trees sway and whine
On avenues
In this forgotten city.
Mostly in shadow now, this great
Hulk of ruin
Hovers darkly. Around it, cold waters
Swirl and flow.
A castle for grasses and plantain weeds,
Fallen towers   open to the sky,
Facing away,
The shell of a waning moon,
A darkening rim.
The old dust will get older on the crumbling wall.
The lichens and mosses deepen
On the ruined stone.

THE LAST CASTLE OF ZAUZOMANK

Stars gaze down on tangled clumps of shrub and vine,
On dew touched leaves the bright drops outline,
On the shadowy forms of
Lichen covered stone,
On ghosts of flowers along a path that's
Little known.
From a cliff falls a rock into the deep shadow below,
Or was that a part of sleep?
Beyond the last forgotten lair
Of fox, of badger, lynx or bear,
There climbs a path, a meandering stair
To ruined walls of darkness where
The faded shades stand rank on rank
To guard the last tower of Zauzomank.
Beyond that lofty tower there rise
Soaring cliffs neath star lit skies.
Those cliffs be ever so far away,
So past the dark tower, there is no way,
But the men of the lord have little need
For more than a shadowy fork for feed,
A shadowy horn for moonlight mead,
For work in the dark, a shadowy creed.
So, walk up the path through shadows and vine,
Through soughing oak and whispering pine.
There is a secret shadows keep:

There's nothing prettier than sleep.
High in the trees they whisper and whine,
There's nothing more beautiful than sleep.
So walk up the path nor fear to wake,
But know that a dawn will never break,
And know that for always a shadowy rank
Stands guard for the Earl of Zauzomank.

THE SILENT CASTLE

On these bare rocks
Above this cold and flowing river
There is no white castle
with red pennants
Flying
Only th.e dark gnarled trees
Sigh in the wind
Blowing.
It isn't there the white bridge
Arched high over the flowing river.
Only the white clouds
Flow over the hill
forever

CAMELOT

From fields of grass, tall monuments
Sweep skyward, tall castle towers
In curves and arcs rise to the heavens
Throwing huge dark shadows on the grass.
The winds that sing and sigh among the
Top most parts seem winds that
Blow among the stars.
The many silent windows, tall and dark,
Are night filled eyes that
Hold vast seas and waters dark,
Are night filled hooded faces looking down,
Dark faces filled with eyes that hold vast seas and waters
dark
In cavities and caves.
Windy fingers move among the towers.
They pass and come again
Through the endless hours.

QUEEN OF THE GLITTERING HEIGHT

The leaves are fallen now and lie
Upon the cooling earth and we remain
To seek the glittering height where
Bright crystals reflect the light
Under the fading white sky.
There is but a mountain path
A stony stair leads up to end in air
And this is the lonely mountain top.
You've scaled the cliffs and, far below
The clouds, you've left the crowds
That cheered an age ago. Now you know
That all the laughter, and the tears,
All the cheers, were lent you for a
Few short years. And short they seem,
As unreal as some pale fading dream,
Some ghostly wing receding, some sinking
Ripple on the surface of a stream.
A queen, you stand atop the stair,
On the final square, in blinding light and
Thinning air and far below
Is every sea and every shore.
Light is here, and air.
You are the Queen of Light and Air,
For there is nothing more. –

THE FLOATING IN DREAM

The ice would crack slightly.
It wouldn't move
Not one second further
Through time.
The sky with the sort of clouds
Would colour the ice
A wet grey.
One could be certain
The grass would be uncut.
One could see it there
Curled beneath the ice.
The ice would lie
A long patch surrounded
By speckled, tramped on snow.
One would see it again in a dream
As a fish
That swims in and out
And mirrors itself
On sleep.

THE SINGING BIRDS OF RHIANNAN

In the wavery silvergrey mists,
In the first winds of morning,
The lemon birds sing.
Green lilies weep the wet dew as they
Wave their tall stalks in the
Wet push of the wind
Nod nodding their swelling green buds
Among the bone pale crosses.
Glittery ochre bees,
In the trees' greenish hidden flowers,
Worry the gold pollen
Which falls in cascading showers
Over the white crosses,
Over the dark earth,
Till it disturbs the bones' black dust.
Then out speaks Heilyn,
"Sit we here feasting, while all these dead
Lie not dark in their graves? Shame on my beard
If I don't open that door. "
And the sun rises casting out greygreen,
Vee and wye shadows of branches to the waiting earth
And the waterwinds, mixed with the
Wild singing, blow in the dark dust till it too
Becomes mixed with the wild singing;
And singing orange rind, sun rising songs,
The lemon birds sing.

THE DOORS OF HENVELYN

In the wavery slivergrey mist
Among the green vee and wye shadows of trees,
In the early winds of sunrise,
Singing fruit and flower sun rising songs.
The lemon birds sing;
Till the mist, mixed with the wild singing,
Floats away from where flowers
Nod. Nodding on their stalks
In the wet push of the wind, nod
Over scattered bones.
Then spake Heilyn,
"Sit we here feasting
While all these dead
Lie not, as they should,
Dark in their graves,
Buried among their venerable ancestors.
Shame on my beard if I do not
Open the doors.
And the winds blew through the
Grey dome of the sky
And all the old troubles of the world
Fell upon those faces
Gathered in the halls of Henvelyn.
And the birds flew away.

THE SHADOW OF THE TUCKAHOE

The ghost of a white river flows over and over
The Beallsville Gardens, the crumbling
Tombstones on the hill over Beallsville.
Through the dark,
The shining wide and flowing pour;
The never ending night and silence
Turn and flow:
The shadow of Tuckahoe.
Above the curved pale outline of the
Standing stones,
Daylight moons rooted darkly in cold clay,
The shining wide pour at the turn,
The long sadness shifting flow,
The white ghost of a pale river,
The shadow of Tuckahoe.
Through from end to end of night,
A recollected chill,
A vaguely remembered dream
Over a high hill,
The depths of that shining shade
Shift and flow:
The shadow of
The Tuckahoe.

NUMBERED AMONG
THE BEALLSVILLE GARDEN

Numbered among the gardens, near the
Moss of that vague patterned path of ruined brick,
This spirit's garden shall lie. Here the
Coarse wire grass and young leaves of Virginia creeper
Are over red clay,
Which shall be covered by
A blanket of of the shadow of the hill
Until the hill shall creep away.
Here shall it linger, this space of the spirit's garden,
On past the day that the stones and the vines
Shall sink away.
Over that cubicle of past
Hung under the
Drifting grey waters, the shadow of the monocacy,
Shall the long sleeve of the wind
Through many a bright hour, play;
Until the air, having had its hour in the light,
Shall fade away.
What the shadow shall know,
As the space of the garden is wrapped in its cradle of
stars,
Is of a dawn covered mountain of snow
And that up and down the Yougohomeny
And from the grey warping piers of the Choptank,
And the sassafras,

The white sails billow as the little breezes blow.
What the shadow shall know,
As it rocks in that tireless cradle of stars,
Is of the little ships that sail past
The little river water towns
On the Nanticoke,
On the Pokomoke,
On the Tuckahoe.
Numbered among the Beallsville gardens, the white sails
Of the Nanticoke,
Of the Tuckahoe.

At the Monococy River Cemetery, Beallsville, Maryland

Far Off Ships That Sail Upon the Sea

The wind blows free
And sweeping always out before,
I see the sea.
The crow call's faint upon the plain.
From a sleepy tree
Flows a sleepy shade.
All's quiet.
Now ships glide silently across an aqua sea.
They are from nowhere,
Going nowhere.
Time calls.
And now I sit beneath a different tree
Yet I still see
In memory
The ships that sail across the sea.
They are from nowhere,
Going nowhere

SONG FOR THE MOON QUEEN

On Linden Hill a lady sits,
A lady in a tree.
Indeed, I love a fair lady
And she, in a far countrie.

UNDER THE BOUGHS

One by one the trees unfold
Bright new leaves of greenery,
Now underneath their boughs are told
The secrets of a summer day,
Underneath their hanging boughs
Are secrets woven day by day.

Two Moons Together Fly

The sky is pale with fleeting light. It's nights' end.
The globe of white is the moon's rising:
The dark begins to fade. The shadows linger in the glade.
The airy light seeps in.
Far way, the plaintive coo of morning doves in the dark
And the dew.
Through the still air it comes again.
The pale, lost echo's on the breeze.
The globe concealed among the trees
In this night's dying.
A golden sickle, globe of white;
In a streaky, cloud mist, pale with light;
With floating space, ever in flight:
Flying moon and flying night.

THE MOON TO POOLESVILLE

As I wandered over a little rise of a dark field,
Past doubled shadows along the downward sloping lane,
The corners of wild bushes waving into indefinite weeds;
Past a warped post falling onto the rutty ground;
As I wandered past the high weeds beside the downward
curving lane,
On a dark hill
I saw the Moon to Poolesville.
I saw the Moon to Poolesville opening its doors.
There on a dark way,
A man was there swinging his lantern
Which cast a flickering light as he limped up the hill
To ride on the Moon to Poolesville;
And I followed him on a little path which I found there,
wavering and still.
On a secret path, he limped up the hill.
He limped up the hill, swinging his lantern light
And leading me onward through the darkening night.

QUICKLY TOO QUICKLY

It was on a bright morning.
Softly I came, It was on a bright morning.
I have forgotten, perhaps there was snow.
I am sure there was laughter.
I think they were flying
Bright coloured kites up into the blue;
But then, It was surely the world that was flying,
No one of us caring where it would go.
What ever would come,
We accepted it gladly:
The day, always young; the sun, shining brightly.
What ever was done, it was always done quickly.
But all of it quickly was carried away.
Now thinking gently
And not without yearning,
It seemed we were always on a bright morning.
Then there were shadows,
I think, without warning.
Now here, you are sleeping,
And I will not stay.

SPRING BEAUTY

Turn around fair maiden and behold
The sparkling spring.
Within their nests of dripping dew the
The singing birds now sing.
Turn, turn on your flowery mound
Amongst anemone and hepatica covered ground.
But for the likes of finch and wren
She would find herself alone
Though bees, at times, on bloodroot flowers
Serenade her with their drone
And then, at times, the mockingbirds
Will sing still music to the day
Or on a clear star sprinkled morn
Its loops of song will whistle away,
Turn turn with your turning year
That your dark eye and ear might see and hear.
There among the mocking birds,
Their feathers and their frills of song,
Sprouting goes our Lady Spring.
Greenery she walks among.
Turn turn in your lonesome grave,
For in the spring breezes the
Spring flowers wave wave

YELLOW LAMPS IN THE MORNING CALM

A night of thunder and rumble
Bright with hundreds of flares
Then toward the dawn,
The noise gets fainter, farther away,
Fades out.
Suddenly the still dawn.
Pale pink, ice covered peaks
Stand tall against the cold grey northern sky.
High above, the wind catches the last
Few flares left by the night
And floats them high over the ice covered peaks
Like yellow balloons.
Distant clanging guns
Like receding thunderstorm.
The sky lightens.
Three floating lamps
Left hanging o'r the horizon.
Red and orange on the clouds' black undersides,
Red ripples on a black wave.
Cloud dragons wind wreath like.
Pale pink, tissue paper peaks
Etched against the northern grey
Like transparent ghosts.
Three floating lamps
Remind me there are other ghosts,
Other than the cold, transparent mountains
In the ebbing dawn.

He Who Was Meant For The East

You with eyes of long meadows and tall pines,
Of the deep waters,
Face of clouds and drifted snow,
You belong to the eastern lands
Only you did not know.
You who would not stay and could not go,
You who were once violent,
Whose flame and dare and laughter
Whose rage shook the east
Are now huge quiet eastern mountains.
Your voice is the slow wind.
In the cool dawn
Cloud dragons decorate your brow.
Rest peacefully,
Rest peacefully, deep waters, twisted pines -

GHOSTLY MEMORY

She recalled a handsome soldier
And indeed, he did look fine.
Set beside him was a bottle
Out of which he poured her, wine.
Vaguely, he'll appear in memory,
Cheerfully, upon a chair,
Gaily talking, joking, drinking
Under darkly waving hair.
When they finished off the bottle;
Sadly, fate he did deplore
That he only had his mustache,
Had his clothes, but nothing more.
On a Sunday, they went walking.
He was dark and he was tall
And he had indeed a mustache.
Nothing else could she recall.
But demand, he did, to kiss her.
When he spoke, each trite cliché
Babbled sweetly in the breezes,
Took a wing and flew away.
Faintly, to disturb her slumber,
Trumpets blared to greet the dawn.
Rank on rank the soldiers gathered
In her dreams, and then were gone.
Leaving but a nameless shadow.

What he wore, it wasn't clear;
But for sure, he had a mustache
And for that, she shed a tear.

THE DARK CHAMPION

Bronze lions roar.
Yellow chariots race.
Strong men on a sun swept floor
Meet other men of courage, skill,
and grace.
Silent vultures soar.
Fingers of dark shadows creep.
Chiefs and champions call for more
fiery wine
Before their draught
of sleep.
He carries the helm which at noontide
he wore.
Flames from the torches leap.
On the stone stair down, he slips on the gore
Of one whose dark eyes fill
with tides of sleep.
His footsteps echo on a stony floor.
He walks on a pace
Toward a dark, hooded man behind a door.
A long black glove will gently
brush his face.
A long black glove
will touch
his face.

THE FACE OF THE STILL WATER

I look into the pool.
I make faces at the water's face.
I say foolish at the water—and an echo answers fool.

I look into the spring,
I see the whispers on the waters lips-
No fears the waters there dispel.
To the listening ears 'tis this, 'this this,
'Tis this whispered;
'Tis only this told:
Death is always careless.
Death is cold.
Death is light as drifting water vapor.
Death is all.
Is transparent as still water,
Swift as falling water,
Swiftly as waters fall.
Hasty fingers yet are careless.
Careless lips will fail.
As a fleeting echo frailest,
As gently sinking sail.
Gently touch the cup of silver to the water cool
That you not diturb the smooth face on the pool.
A single time the water drips
Will share a tremor, a tremor on the lips.

At a splash the waters skin
Breaks and the waters blood, the blood goes out and in.
Each ripple, a shaft of light breaks through,
Breaks through the eye, the cold eye of blue.
'Tis thus the wavery clear green hair
Will into floating tatters tare.
Drink, drink lightly, long and cool,
But do not mar – the
surface of the pool.

THE BLACKBERRY MAN

The past is the present.
And I see Papa,
In a blackberry patch,
His purple hands,
And wagging his chin to think
What all the children are
Talking about.
"There was a time, I was a giant   with a cigar
In a rattan chair
Puffing smoke at
Bolo waving Igerotes,
All over the Philippines,
With a one eyed bishop
And a Chinese doctor
At my elbow.
They call me the Blackberry man
Now....."
I closed my eyes
And I saw Papa,
His many thoughts all over his mind,
The purple juice all over his hands,
A one eyed bishop,
A black patch over his eye,
And a Chinese doctor.

THE BLUE LAMP AND THE GREEN

The committee for the distribution of properties
Was in accord, said the visitor, that the
Chairman of the Ohio delegation should be
Awarded a green lamp and a blue lamp
For his private use. The chairman
Was out in his garden plucking hairy green
Gooseberries when he got the news.
And he was thinking of things his delegation
Had done, while he plucked
Black dewberries, and russet wineberries,
To go with the gooseberries,
and dark currants fell into his pot.
Then the visitor had come. There was a click.
The visitor had, on his way out, shut the gate.
Footsteps patted on the path, faded.
The activities of the delegation had been
Hardly more exciting than their dry talk
And that rush of angel wings. Yes, there had been
Little excitement among the members of the delegation.
The one surprise, the governor had arrived unexpectedly
To join them here; had then convinced one third (of the
angels)
That his claims against God were correct. Here
Was a dead frog under the arrowwood vibernum. It
would

Be stiff and slimy to the touch.
Groaka groaka. Another frog croaked down by the
Pool. The governor opposed the other republicans
With no small degree of success. It was the
Little things which seemed to fall his way. He
Found advantage in the marriage of the
Daughter of Charibert, king of Franks Incorporated,
And then there were the thrones and them that
Sat upon them, and the ghosts of them that were
Beheaded for the witness of the past. His degree of
Success, thought the chairman, rendered him and
His exploits so large an argument of romance
That history would, to a great degree, disclaim both.
The delegation had favored Kemp for the
Second spot on the ticket. The governor
Preferred Bush. Now the visitor had
Made available the two lanterns
For the chairman to use.
The blue lantern, the visitor had said,
The chairman would likely use several times,
There would be, perhaps, a score of times,
It would be found useful.
The visitor said it was not likely
The chairman would use the green lantern.
No, it was most unlikely
He would ever use the green at all.

TAKING DOC OUT OF DOC

Doc emptied his glass. Big fat Mr. Porter
Filled it up. It was a standard brand, but
For Doc, poisonous. Doc took a sip,
Picked up his cigar. A little blue man
Came out of the drink. The
Genie of the glass: screwed off the top of
Doc's head. Doc took a worried puff on
His cigar; puffed out smoke while the genie
Pulled out half an el of blue sky,
Out of Doc's head, pulled out a field of
Happy sad unsmiling people, pulled out the masks
Of long benign contented thoughts
So that the light bulb glared on but half
Of Doc's face. His thoughts drifted off on
The other half.
And the genie
Got on a wagon of barrels; said "I'm going to
Drive slow so you won't be too hard pushed
When you follow. " And so I
Went under a tree so the long limbs
Would shade my face.
So that the sun wouldn't embarrass my face.
But the genie really wasn't there.
Only the poisonous liquid in the glass. Only
The cigar, the smoke, the tablespoon ladling out

The pictures from Doc's smoke: the
El of sky, the field of people and the masks
Of thoughts.
And Doc was puffing
Smoke and I was out along the road
Hearing the dogs bark and
Wondering what they were
Talking about:
The dogs bark and along the bend in the
Dusty road; past the split logs fencing the
Bushes and boulders of a meadow, past the
Rickety grey boards of a tumbled down
Milk stand in a patch of dusty nettles, rattles the
Wagon of barrels. Down the road go the
Huge hoofed, Black Clydesdale horses, the
Blue genie seated on top of the barrels with
The half el of sky, the field, the masks, the
Many hidden peculiar things that
Gone forever, are
Shaking in.
Now far off along the vacant road
All the dogs bark.

The Street of Yesterday

There were streets of yesterday,
Alleyways which never reached the sun.
Ox carts ground the cobblestones.
All these, paved over and gone.

There were streets of yesterday,
Avenues where shaking shadows spun.
On silver leaves the gas lamps shown.
All these, built over and gone.

There were streets of yesterday,
Twisting lanes with brambles over run.
The crickets chirped in undertones.
All these, grown over and gone.

I found a road of yesterday,
Of ruts and rocks, which ancient shadows cast.
I followed it. On either end,
It faded out and led into the past.
On that winding road I'll stray,
That hidden way where ends are never seen,
But lead to a million yesterdays
On silent moon paths
Which lie there
Peaceful, undisturbed, serene.

Song For The Dying Wind

From silvery night to the moonlit day
I came, swished past and sailed away,
Bathed in a shadowy silvery day,
We breezes blow where   old trees sway.
Here I was carried away   away
Into the green glow and blue gloom.
All day long you may look to find
Where we winds sing low in the ivies twined;
Then: search, as you sleep the long night through,
Your troubled dreams come back to you;
But never a trace of old   wind you see,
Though younger wind flies from tree to tree
While moonlight washes a silent dew
On the old paths where   we winds blew.
With flying cloud, in the evening grey,
I came, swished past and sailed away.
O I was carried away away
Through the green glow and blue gloom.
Though you walk ever so far away,
Though long through the dark night, dream you may;
You never will find, in the night or day,
Where we were carried, where we winds play;
Where I was carried away away
Into the green glow and blue gloom.
But the clouds that flew and the green trees knew,

And the cold and moonlit hills of blue;
Where I was carried away away
Through the green glow and blue gloom.
Fading now into the cool deep,
While times dark shifting tides over me sweep,
While a sad wind is whining to sleep,
I will be   carried away.

WIND TOSSED SHADOWS

Falling leaves blow away
They are seldom asked to stay
Ask a shadow in to tea
For there is no guarantee
That tomorrow you and I
Won't be shadows on the fly.

There will be some windy day
I will have turned a shade of grey,
Blowing wind will shake my tree,
Then a swish and I'll be free.
If you see my shadow pass
Don't turn down an empty glass.

Whispering leaves are light and dry.
With the wind they flutter by.
Should a shade drop in to dine
Give it spirit of the vine.
Should it blow into your knook
Put it in your shadowbook.

ADVANCE OF THE TALL TWISTERS

Away Away Away
Across the horizon, I see them coming.
In the distance rise tall dark columns of twisting air.
Twisting columns advance.
Behind what dark door do they hide
While the columns are leveling the wild outside,
While the columns are bending and twisting
And leveling the wind outside,
A great father creating a new land,
A land of passion and sorrow,
An unfriendly land.
Do they go out and strive with the winds?
Do they wait
And breathe the air of red roses,
Pale in the moonlight,
Drained of colour in the moonlight
In Halfway House
The place of philosophers grey
Where there are no living roses,
But only the crystal roseghosts
In the garden of Halfway House
Where philosophers are always grey?
Away Away Away
Across the horizon   I see them coming
In the distance rise tall datk columns of twisting air.

Twisting columns advance.
Here is the dark door.
Three jet blue tubes of twisting air,
Tall on the horizon,
Advancing across the blue hills,
Across the fields of corn stubble and wild grasses,
Bending and twisting and leveling the wild outside
A great father creating a new land,
An unfriendly land.
Behind what dark door,
While the columns are leveling the wild outside?
Out and strive with the winds
In that land of passion and sorrow,
In that hard light of that bright grey day?
Behind that dark door are crystal roseghosts
Drained of colour in the moonlight
A memory of moonlight
In Halfway House where, frozen in the moonlight,
Memories of fleeting shadows play
Over endlessly deep waters
In the gardens
Where philosophers are always grey. But wait,
Breathe the air of moonlight
In this not too unfriendly place,
In this place where bloom a profusion of roses,
Pale in the moonlight,
Hanging in the stillness over cool waters
In the gardens of Halfway House
Where philosophers are always grey.

THE WHALES ARE RIDING IN THE SEA

On this blue day the corn is turning golden.
The feathery seeds are blowing ghosts of flowers.
Still through the sighing trees
The dappled sun is warm.
Still through the trees now golden comes
The warmth the Crow requires.
All the whales are riding in the sea,
The black whales through the liquid pass
Oblivious to the changes of the seasons
The ocean rolls on glittery surfaces.
I know these October cornfields where black crows
Peck at the sun ripened grain.
I know the old tale of the slain year
And the spring season when the earth gives back its slain.
I know the whales are riding in the sea
And as the sun weaves dappled patterns
On the forest floor,
I know the tall wind rising in the East
Will allow me to know nothing more.
All the whales are riding in the sea,
So passes each black shadow in the glass.
Still are the tall winds rising in the East.
Still undisturbed, the shadows pass.
The whales are riding in the sea.
One by one their silent shadows pass

Still are the tall winds rising in the East.
Still undisturbed, the shadows pass.
On this blue day the year's becoming olden
In falling leaves and blowing ghosts of flowers.
Still through the sighing trees the
Dappled sun is warm.
Still through the red and yellow leaves,
The warmth all life requires.
All the whales are riding the sea,
The black whales through the liquid pass
Oblivious to the changes of the seasons
The ocean rolls on glittery surfaces.
In know these October cornfields where black crows
Peck at the sun ripened grain.
I know they'll linger, linger in these fields
Until the year is slain.
I know the whales are   riding the sea
And as the sun weaves splotched and mottled
Patterns on the forest floor,
I know the tall wind   rising in the East
Will allow me to know nothing more.
All the whales are   riding in the sea,
One by one their   silent shadows pass.
Still are the tall winds   rising in the East.
Still unperturbed the shadows pass.

Night Storm With Lightning

The lightning flashed. The black field
Was watery white with daisies.
The field was turning. The
Lightning flashed. The field was
Black hands waving, flapping pennant trees.
The lightning flashed. The field was a
White wall, water clear and high.
The field was crying, crying with the wind,
Roaring with the thunder. The shining wall
Swept on. The lightning flashed in rumpled
Pearly clouds, great sails of fire.

AT ALBERT'S COCKTAIL PARTY

At the cocktail party at Alberts
Jane left the large living room
Its contour chairs bright couches potted trees
And abstract art   went into the bathroom
Shiny tile floor bright white bathtub
And toilet opened a mirrored
Medicine cabinet took a bottle from a
Row of bottles on a glass shelf
Drank the contents   one last bath
Jane took off her clothes   started the tub
Filling with cool water   passed out on the
Tile floor.   Albert hearing the
Water running and running
Knocked and knocked   opened the door
Seeing Jane naked on the tile floor
Closed the door   to get Myrna or Nan
Or somebody.   Howell needing to use the
White toilet   opened the door   and there
In front of the white toilet
In front of the chrome and white basin
Tile sloped to a large pool.
Behind the pool   rose a white rock cliff
To the right water trickled over the rocks
In a fall. White flowered water weeds
Waved their arrow shaped leaves at the

Waters edge. Above the pool   on a
Ledge of white rock, reclined a naked girl.
Howell she called I'm here by the pool.
Howell she called I'm here by the pool.
But Howell heard none of this.
His thoughts began as the sentence ended.
His thoughts began as the sentence ended
He heard only   oo ool oo ool
Echoing from the cliffs.
Fantastic bathroom, said Howell,
His voice mingling with the
Falling water   less impressive
He thought the potted trees
The abstract art   in the living room.
A lot less. He turned around
Pissed in the toilet   flushed it
And watched the water swirl around.
He turned and watched the
Clear bright trickle over the rocks
As he buttoned his fly. He heard the
Gurgle of water   as it fell into the pool. There was no
lady on
The white rock ledge. Jane was not there.
Jane was already   far away —

THE CUP AT CARBONEK

The essence floated in the cup.
It drifted like a molten gold,
But one might shake to lift it up,
His heart beat fast, his blood run cold.
At carbonek the weathered stone
Hid among its shadows dark
An ancient cup which held, alone,
An essence from a vernal spark.
That drought insured eternal youth,
The bubbling essence in the cup.
Deadly too, it was, in truth,
For one who dared to drink it up.
Then gossip spread the news around
That famous knights were in the town:
Sir Gilbert and Sir Griflet too,
Sir Neal Hangcock and Sir Hue.
With famous knights so close at hand
A proper welcome there was planned.
Of things made ready for a feast,
That ancient cup was not the least.
The knights desired to have a look.
The cup inspired delight and dred;
For that castle, many took
To be a dwelling for the dead.
Some furtively passed by the door:
Sir Kay, Sir Hector and Sir Tor,

Sir Ontzlake and Sir Pelenore,
Sir Tristram and Sir Sagremore.
In the sunset's fading light
Did patient King Amfortas wait.
Twilight darkened into night,
But no one entered into the gate.
Then came the day a visitor came:
A knight, Sir Parsifal by name
And yes, he'd dine, but then he left
Before he saw the fiery draught.
Then, sadly, each day passed the same,
The uncured king lay quiet and lame.
In the stillness, dust lay deep
And the porters were asleep.
Eternal youth flowed from the cup,
A bubbling vernal season.
The reason one should dred to quaf:
Likewise, it was a poison.
The essence floated in the cup and drifted there
Like molden gold
But if one shook to take it up, though one might
Otherwise be bold, his heart beat fast, his
Blood run cold —
In truth, there was a reason.
The draft insured eternal youth, the fires of Beltane
Burning bright, the first kiss of that
Virgin night in the flower filled season.
To reach that joy these things contain,
One drinks that draught, does not refrain,
Then arms and fights with might and main
The painted Pict the lordly Dane
Then dies and lies beneath the plain.
That essence is a poison.

THE GIRL IN A TEACUP

Hsiao Hu   Little Tiger
Glowing pale bronze face and eyes of jet
Hair, a silky mist of stary night
Girl of the teacup
Queen of the brazen gong
Burn in the lamplight
Under your pale flower tree
Drive your dragons on   little tiger
Girl in the silver tower
Shine in the candle glow
The silver blossoms flower
While stars through the twilight
Knife through the crystal hour
Now yellow dusk
Strange music of sweet dreams
Where under the blossoms the petals fall in streams
Spice sweet notes echo - now fall -
Tea time passes -
The old ones seek their pall little princess -
Templed cities sleep
Stone gods vigil keep
As the people pass
While sacred fires cast reflections
On the garnished brass.
The stone gods sleep and dream

They laugh at the girl in the teacup
By her stream -
Chimes of laughter linger in a dream.
Hsiao Hu   Little Tiger
Girl on the silver tower
Shine in the candle glow -
The silver blossoms flower
While stars through the twilight
Knife through the twisted hour.
The god of a lost sea
Is staring through rose pale time
Where sea shells moan sadly
While the seas cold curled jades chime -
The god of a lost sea
In the gold and red setting sun
Hears the sea shells moan sadly
While the brazen waves thunder and run -
Now yellow dusk -
Strange music of sweet haunted dreams -
Spice fragrant notes echo
Now shrill   now they fall -
Tea time passes, old ones seek their pall.
Little princess, play with your crystal ball.
Watch templed cities
Asleep from the dawn of time
Where old gods stare
At the girl on the temple
And her star filled hair   little princess -
Stone gods ancient watch,
Watch the people pass
While sacred fires reflect on garnished brass,
Ivory monsters, gems and fairy glass.

Now under the blossoms
The petals fall in streams -
Stone eyes slumber on and dream
Tinkling laughter by a stream
Where a lost traveler
Wanders through haunted dream,
A phantom in a phantom dream -

Song of the White Cockrose

The white cockrose over the white lily crows.
In all their pale beds
The lilies loll their heads
Together down the twisty track
Front and back,
Front and back, lily and rose,
White on white, white with dewy glows.
The lilies and the roses wed,
Pale white over a pale bed.
All, in twisted morn
Water a white harp.
Grapes and plums
Fall from a crumpled horn
And apples, green apples.
Clear waterwaves swell from the still spring,
Off is the white moon cover.
She is off with her long legged lover,
Shafty legs, - tall as the sky,
Sugar tongs strides away,
Strides away into the blue,
Into the blue sky.

THE GREAT WHEEL OF ARTHUR IN THE BLUE HEAVENS

In the sky's blue heavens
I saw that great wheel,
King Arthur at his table.
The grey King Uriens at his side,
Tall Kay next to Lord Horns
And Lord West Wind was there.
King Melwas was there from the Land of Summerwhite.
The Green Knight sat next to dark visaged Death.
Next sat Lugh Longspear.
The one eye of Baylor peered over the table.
By him wagged the beard of the Lord of the Woods.
Sir Mighty Grasp sat next,
And angry, red faced Sir Sun was there.

THE PLOW OF ARTHUR'S

I took myself to see the fool
While searching for wise and good.
With me were Lugh Longspear and Kay
And Killer Jack and Old Nick Hood.
Flow, you mighty waters. Blow winds, blow.
I asked him for a silver star.
He smiled as if he understood.
With me were Lancelot of the car
And Bog Demagus of the wood.
Flow, you mighty waters. Blow winds, blow.
A star, I asked. He gave me but a plow.

GUINHYWVARE THE TALL AND FAIR

Guinhywvare, the tall and fair
Daughter of Lord Ogrevan;
Walked, with moonlight in her hair,
Alone where unknown waters ran.
To no god would she offer prayer,
Nor copulate with any man.
A shaft of moonlight touched her hair,
Touched the mist she chose to wear
And fell upon the shining sand,
It threw pale light upon the land
And filled the leaves with sliver where
In the stillness did she stand
Beneath the pendent silver pear,
A bow and arrow in her hand.
To no god would she offer prayer
Nor copulate with any man.
Nor copulate with any man.

THE MAN IN THE MOON AND THE MORNING FAY

The man in the Moon, one cloudy day,
Came down to surprise Morgan the Fay.
He snuck up behind her, gave her a push,
And she fell into a hawthorn bush.
He pinched her titty, he paddled her rear,
He nibbled the bottom of her ear,
He tore her garment, gave her a push,
And she fell into a hawthorn bush.
He pulled her hair, he paddled her rear,
He nibbled the bottom of her ear.

FOR THOSE WHO DIED YOUNG

Pluto was a lusty lad.
Proserpine, a lovely girl.
Pluto's hair was black as jet,
But he loved the golden curl.

Pluto snatched up Proserpine
As she picked an asphodel.
On a jet black horse they rode
Toward a shadowy gate of Hel.

Over waters dark, they passed;
Waters of dark Lethe's stream.
From the Lethe, vapors rose
And put them deep into a dream.
But all that happened yesterday
In meadows near the River Styx
Where lusty lads, still making hay,
Are putting maidens in a fix.

And who are we to sigh or whine
If they, with golden maidens, play
While Death puts Lethe in their wine,
So that they sleep and dream away.

Lovely maidens still pick flowers
That sparkle with the morning dew,
But some of them are wet with tears.
For Proserpine was lovely, too.

THE BOGIEMAN SETS THINGS RIGHT

The stone that was shaped like a house
Danced in the moonlight under the pale lily tree.
"Now does he have to do that?" said the moon.
"It's his nature," said the snow leopard.
"I shall have to ask my Lord Sun," said the moon.
"I have already asked the King Lion
And he said it was all right," said the snow leopard.
"Then there is nothing I can do," said the moon.
"No, it's out of our hands," said the snow leopard.
The stone finished bathing and,
In the little round clearing,
Danced around the toadstools.
The Boogieman came from behind a thorn bush
And said, "do you have to do that?
Look, you have kicked over a toadstool,
The sheep horned man won't like that,
And besides, you've stepped on my boogie hole."
"My feet feel so good they won't stop dancing,"
Said the stone. "Then dance them out of there,"
Said the Boogieman, "There's a clearing over there.
It's got plenty of place to dance in
And there are no toadstool rings to kick over.
And my boogie hole isn't in that clearing."
The Boogieman waved his long feelers,
Pulled his cat whiskers with his hairy paw,

Looked up at the stone,
"And if the sheep horned man eyeballs you
Kicking over anymore toadstools,
He'll likely turn you into a teakettle.
How would you like that?
Or into, perhaps, a ring-tailed moocow.
How would that grab you?
It'd be a weird scene, wouldn't it?"
The stone danced over to the other clearing.
"I might have thought of that myself,"
Said the moon.

SONG OF THE BLACK LIGHT BRAILLE

I went in at this crazy way out dance
A swinging time was happening
An obscene, now type thing
Like wow, man, it was where it was
Everyone switched onto this
Fun groove and the freaked out groupies digging it
I mean
Getting with it; like, knocked out. It was their bag,
A stone gas.
Then too, the rest of the crowd was sort of neat, A lot a
heads
Getting it on, and like laying on us their
Out a sight raps.
I mean, into trips you could really dig on.
The vibrations,
Pretty heavy stuff.
The younger children making the scene
Were drinking some, but they kept it
Pretty well together.
And we knew where they were coming from.
And if that's where their heads were at,
It was cool.
The bikers there didn't off them, though they
Had, I suppose, their
Knives and chains; but together we tripped on

What was going down.
Then, through the electric scream, through the
Blue haze of smoke, on the place itself, and that
Flat ass
Blew us away. I mean sculptures,
Spaced art on the walls,
Bottle filled bar and obscenely huge chairs
In the corners.
Some trip. Heavy. And, as
Part of the decoration, the ever present
Fuzz were there. Hired by management of course.
So, short of murder, weren't going to dismantle themselves
From the rest of the scenery, put the
Paying customers up tight,
Nor discourage the people from huffing and puffing,
But it'd be strictly uncool should some cat
Try and cop
Where the fuzz would just have to eyeball him.
Or had his stash out in plain sight. I mean, had
Some dude
Gotten himself busted, it'd been a
Drag for everybody.
A real down. The
Gittings HaHa had been supplying the sound. A
Tough outfit; but not expected
If you know what I mean,
To be blowing people's minds.
But they were doing their thing
And the people were
Digging them in anticipation of
Better things to come.
The HaHa was packing its stuff away and some

Blacklight Braille was
Taking the stand.
A weird scene. It had the people
Bent out of shape.
And everybody was saying
"Where's James? Where's the Choptank? Did they split?
Oh, man!"
The Blacklight Braille set up.
"Life's for the action," the
Lean faced singer sang.
He waved his golden hair.
Sounds crashed in red and gold lights'
Alternating flare.
"Quit crying girl, work out for kicks. Do you dare? Oh,
do you dare?
James sang in this place last night,
Then, through the back door,
He slipped out into the dark.
Tonight let me sing to you instead.
Flash the strobe lights. Let the wild
Waves rock.
James sang here, then late last night,
Something wasn't cool.
He slipped in his red blood's spilling pool.
He stepped out on the darkness of
The starlit road,
Out into the darkness his naked feet
Have gone
To meet along the darkness of the
Starlit road,
The years at the Turn. The years at the Turn.
The years at the Turn."

LAST CALL

The call of the horn is the summons
It is the wild hunt
Rushing forth from the heart of darkness
From the primal midnight,
Led by Wotan himself
Riding the Ghost Way
With the baying of wind hounds and the wild cries of
warriors
Echoing through the sky as they pass over.
It is the way my father took,
My father's father before him.
It is the summons
Calling us to ride
To merge with the spirit hunt,
The ghostly dead warriors in the spirit place
Of no time, which is all time.
In that place which is no place.
It is the call
to draw us into that – ghostly way
Where the order of our time and space
Sinks into chaos.
It is the call heard by my fathers
It is the road of my fathers.
Hail, Wotan.

HE TOLD JACKSON

I found Jackson in a hard, bitter land
Where little that is green would grow
And that, that grew, more grey than green
And, as we listened to the bald wind blow,
I told Jackson that his home, the city of
His youth, that once we two beheld as
Fair as Heaven, was crumbled and dirtied,
Marble towers fallen and dark as
Trampled February snow.
Jackson said it wasn't so.

OLD CINCINNATI

A churchlike structure, on ninth and vine,
Of brick, that was ancient and worn;
Was where, in the shadows, the dirty old men
Waited to watch soft porn.
Inside, old men started shouting for beer
As sweet little Lil showed the crack in her rear.
The men in the back were the first to cheer
As the girls revealed their thighs.
Up front, their hands in their pockets, the men
Looked up, showed mild surprise,
Then hasted out the ceiling lights
With buttons off their flies.
Old pruneface, the usher, stood by the door.
As he watched the feathers that the girls wore,
His grey wrinkled foreskin expanded once more;
He felt old Peterskin rise.
Some baldheaded men were shouting for beer
As sweet Hattie showed them the crack in her rear.
The man wearing glasses was starting to cheer
The shaking, plump, naked thighs.
Texas Star toyed with the horn of a steer.
The bald men bugged out their eyes;
Then, blasted out the ceiling lights
With buttons off their flies.

THE REVENUERS

We saw them standing
At the Newport Landing.
All the dogs in town were barking
To let us know the revenuers
Had come here.
We saw them standing
At the Newport Landing,
All the dogs in town were barking,
"Protect your cigarettes and beer."
We saw them standing
at the Newport Landing.
All the dogs in town were barking
to let us know that they were here.
We saw them standing
At the Newport Landing.
All the dogs in town were barking,
"Protect your beer."

THE BUTT END OF OUR DAY

There's a chuckle down a cobbled lane
A wrinkled face peeks through a dirty pane.
There's a lad astride a ragged broom
Clear the way, the lad's demanding room
Between the stones, the sinking flame is dim
Brooding crows sit on a leafless limb
Feathery clouds ride through endless grey
An old man has left and gone away
Somewhere distant barking can be heard
A ratty looking cat has killed a bird
Burnt log ends fall into the wind
There's a flicker over sooty stone
Music over, these old lips are dumb
From the dark the creeping shadows come
Quietly quietly now the day will end
Old logs fall and fall into the wind.

AT THE PITS

That's the pit, the subway they call it.
No, I don't know where it goes.
And I wouldn't crawl in there if I were you.
They call this place 'The Pits,'
But there's only one.
No, that one is filled with water.
Now, through these brambles. Yes, see?
It has water in it. See there go the
Most marvelous fish, always twenty.
You may count them if you wish.
See how shiny silver - count them as they go.
In and outthe lili pads – and long teeth
See how their bottom jaws stick out? Over there?
Those ruined stones? That's the
Boogie Man's Tower. I remember it standing.
Ancient and lopsided. That was way before
Your time. I was about so high,
Remember seeing scraggly white haired old men,
Three of them. End of a most ancient line,
They said. And there were twenty fish back then.
And the men, gaunt, white haired, terribly wise.
Yes, I imagine they did get sorta cold
What did they say? They said
Life was brief. They said the fish were –
Pretty old.

DEATH OF A BAG

April fool's for funny men,
A funny man is Mr. Clown
Who filled a bag with water
And dropped it on the ground.
He smiled and gave his head a wag
And said, "the earth is now a bag."
All through April and through May
I watched the ground on which it lay.
Every day I looked, I found
That it looked more like the ground
And then early in the fall,
I could discern no bag at all.
Then, April Fool's Day came to mind
Through out the windy woods I'd find
Laughter in the shrubs and trees.
The words they whispered were but these,
As they shook their heads with mirth,
"The Earth's The Bag, The Bag The Earth."

At The Foot of The Stairway

In the dark hall, at the foot of the stairway,
There lies a man with silver eyes
And all the dancing table legs.
The sun and the moon will grow much less,
Two hats hang on fat pegs.
The lonely room will wander there
Beside the moonless night.
The moon and a jumping cannon ball
Begin to bark and bite.

WHY THE NIGHT IS CROSSED

Why the night is crossed with lying tree trunks
With the greyness falling, rising, with a motion
Of fungus forest flying
A wiggling es of white foretells a sad fate,
Swings in and out, a bent pipe from grey to grey.
There, a flight of crows grows smaller, leaving.
Here, a wall of pink heads smiling
With an ease of coffin hinges falling
Sing their message to the hanging morning.
This is just a path of burning jockstraps.
This is just a pool of whistling eyes.
This is just a feeling from the evening.
This is just a common living failing –

GWYN MILL

Turn wheel turn
The hoary water churn
Churn the hoary brook water
With the grey green slimy wheel.
By the green banks of fern
Turn wheel turn.
Grind the wheat and rye.
Grind John Barleycorn
And the lads who are climbing up Sugar Hill,
And the babe that's just been born.
Howard and jack got around in the mill
Along with their carrots and corn.
Turn wheel turn
Turn wheel
Squeak squeal
Grind creak
Sag leak
Roll reel
Grind meal
Grate shriek
Grind creak
Turn
Wheel
Turn
Wheel
Turn
Wheel
Turn––

ALONE ON A ROCK

Walking along a tangled path
In a forgotten place,
I saw a man upon a rock
Seated in that waste.
Far away, the pale moon shown over a distant hill.
It turned him to a silhouette; he, sitting there so still.
"Old man," I said,
"Why are you here in this dreary place?"
Then, he turned and looked at me.
He hadn't any face.

THE YEW IN WINTER

While we in winter come to frozen breath,
Under the ice, the Yew makes truce
With Death.
In spring, to keep its promise
With the Yew,
Earth reforms to give love
Breath anew;
But we, not knowing where our
Lost Sun's gone;
Toward the Earth must keep
Moving on,
And when we leave, the promise
To the Yew
Demands that Earth be kind
And Death be true.

NIGHT SHAPES

A circle of a moon, lemon white; a black
Circle of a moon;
An el shaped cloud of lusterous pearl;
A black el shaped cloud;
And a dark, brownish black triangle
Of jutting stone;
A white triangle;
And a dark, bluish form of God on the horizon;
A White God

DEATH MASK

There I see
Your mask upon the wall.
There I see
The lights about you fall.
Stars wheel down,
The skies become your shroud.
Gone long since
Are bird   and tree and cloud.
Far away
The wind does blow and blow and blow.
Now I see
The night has come to scowl.
Now I hear
The wind has come to howl.
Your hollow words
Are echoes in a well
Heard before
The lights about you fell.
Now I see
The sheet that is your shawl.
Now I see
Your mask upon the wall.

CALENDAR

Jan 1 - New Year's Day - Angonia of Janus D. Robert the Strong

Jan 4 - B. Jacob Grimm - B. Isaac Newton

Jan 5 - Koreion - Berchtas Eve - Latonas Eve

Jan 6 - Epiphany - Virzkirszt - Theophania - Sirona

Jan 10 - Day for Geraint the Blue Bard

Jan 11 - Juturna - Carmentalia - B. Theodosius I

Jan 12 - Distaff Day – Compitalia, Frigg Honoured

Jan 13 - Tiugunde - Lenaia - Proerosia, Day for Teu - Knut
Honoured

Jan 18 - Sires Eve - Theodorus Fest

Jan 19 - Thorablotar Thor Honoured - Cerdic Honoured

Jan 20 - Yngona Randolf Flambard Honoured

Jan 24 - B. Frederick Der Grossa

Jan 25 - Old Disting - Robert Burns Day

Jan 27 - Sementivae Feria - Scathachs Day

Jan 28 - Up Helly AA Lady Mourne Oglanny Honoured –
Widukind - D. Sir Francis Drake - King Bagsac

Jan 31 - Day for Queen Adeliza - B. Franz Schubert

Feb 1 - Imbolc - Brigantia - Princess Hervors Day - Hlathguth
Swanwhite - Hothversdottir Olrun Valkyrie of Wales - King
Egbert I Crowned

Feb 2 - Candlemas - Kerzemesse - Groundhog Day - Februa -
Gondul the Valkyries Day - Queen Penthesileias Day -
D. King Sweeney - D. Dunstan the Smith

Feb 5 - Wyrd Day - Tyche Day

Feb 7 - Mabsant Fest - Richard the Lionheart

Feb 11 - Anthesteria - Chytrori

Feb 12 - Cunobelines Day - B. Thomas Campion

Feb 14 - Valentine - Granus Fire - Lycaea - Venus - Vali - Rind - Grian - Graine - Cupid - Queen Libuse – Battle Maiden Lilliard of Ancrum - Sigrun Hognisdottir - King Helgi - Lady Irpa - Matilda of Mobray - Catullus

Feb 15 - Lupercalia - Lupercus - Goddess Amalthea - Pan - Diva Augusta Faustina Honoured

Feb 21 - Biiken Fire - Feralia - Charista - Purity Day - Lord York Celebrated

Feb 22 - Eboracum - Washington's Birthday - George Washington

Feb 23 - Terminalia - Queen Dwyanned Fest

Feb 24 - Regifugium

Feb 27 - Selene Fest - D. Tarquin King of Rome - D. King Siga

Mar 1 - Whuppity Stourie - Matronalia - Davids Day - Juno - Modron - Lady Creidne

Mar 2 - Chad Day - Ceadda Nimue of Llyn Fawr - Dragon Queen Nessa - King Sighere

Mar 3 - Storms Day - Aegir Day Rhiannon Fest - Lear - Iduna - Bragi Boddasson Honoured - D. Battle Leader Lady Martna Glar

Mar 5 - B. Frederick I Barbardsa

Mar 8 - D. Grainne Ni Malley - Sverre Sigurdsson

Mar 11 - D. Queen Lampeto - D. Witch Margaret Flower

Mar 15 - Equirria - Mars - Danu - Anna Perenna - Macha - D. Julius Caesar - Lady Synoppe

Mar 17 - Agonium Martiale - Marzanna - Liberalia - Patricks Day - Mars – Libera, Aife

Mar 18 - Lucarium - Sacred Groves Fest - Athene - Warrior Queen Velda - Queen Hariasa - D. Edward the Saxon

Mar 19 - Quinquatrus - Minerva - Quirinus - Mars - Warrior
Queen Marchel - Queen Gwenliana of Kidwely - D. Eyvind
Kinnrifi - Queen Lathgertha - D. Alexander III King of
Scotland

Mar 20 - B. Ovidius Naso Publius - D. Duncan Ban Macintyre

Mar 21 - Tea and Tephi Day - Tara Founding - Queen Tea -
Queen Tephi - Aonghus OC - Becuma Queen of Earth
Cairbre Queen Suvetar - Poet Lady Uallach - B. Augusta Lady
Llanover - B. Johann Sebastian Bach

Mar 23 - Tubilustrum - Nerine Day - Heimdal Fest - Nerine
Mars

Mar 24 - Priestess Gladus Brychansdottir

Mar 25 - Lady Day - Cailleach Day - Bellona's Day - Black
Agnes - Rhea - Hippolyte - Marpesia - Lady Semiramis -
Mary Read - Otrere - Hippo Queen Galswinth - D. Turlough
Ocarolan - D. Robert Bruce - Queen Sexburga of Wessex -
Queen Gerberge - Empress Triaria

Mar 27 - D. James VI King of Scotland

Mar 28 - Warrior Goddess Rheda Honoured - Ragnar Lodbrok
Victory at Paris - Viking Lady Alfhild Siwardsdottir

Mar 31 – Luna Fest

Apr 1 - April Fool - Aphrodite Day - Skadi Macedonian Witch
Phyllis Honoured - D. Eleanor Aquitaine - B. Otto Von
Bismarck

Apr 2 - Flowers Battle - Lady Cetnenn Day

Apr 6 - Delphinia - Apollo Purification

Apr 7 - B. William Wordsworth

Apr 8 - Mounichia - Iphegenia Day - Artemis Fest

Apr 9 - Lady Rheada the Warrior Victory - Hakon the Great
Sigurdsson

Apr 10 - Musician Lady Hedea Victory at Games

Apr 13 - D. Arthur I King of Brittany

Apr 14 - D. Georg Friedrich Handel

Apr 15 - Cerelia - Fordicidia - Sommarnatt - Tellus Day - Ceres
- Proserpine - Tellus

Apr 16 - B. Aphra Amis Behn Priestess of Easter

Apr 17 - Easter - Aurora - Andraste - Lady Otrere - Queen
Boudicca Honoured - D. Justin I Emperor of Rome -
B. Thomas Vaughan - B. Henry Vaughan

Apr 20 - Floralia Flora - Queen Tanaquil - D. Ceadwallader

Apr 21 - Parilia - Arbor Day - Birth of Rome - Pales - Pallas
- Vesta - Romulus - Remus

Apr 22 - Plenteria - D. Witch Ruth Osborne

Apr 23 - Green George Day - Shakespeare Fest – Green Man
Day - Dragon Honoured - William Shakespeare - D. Brian
Boru - D. Ethelred the Unready

Apr 25 - Robigalia - Cuckoo Day - Lady Robigo

Apr 26 - D. Alfred the Great - B. Marcus Aurelius - D. Wihtred
King of Kent

Apr 28 - D. King Rhys Ap Gruffydd

Apr 29 - Alade Mystae - King Urien Memoria Ceridwen -
Arawn

Apr 30 - Beltane - Walpurgisnacht - Freinacht Drudennacht -
Bechuille Belinus - Carman - Robin Goodfellow - B. Taliesin
- Thomas Rhymer Honoured - Meroe the Witch - Perimede
the Witch - Fergus Mac Roich - Flidais Stagmistress - Lord
Odonoghues Ride Into the Lake - D. Hywel Hen

May 1 - May Day - Dippy Day - Maia - Maeve - Pan -
Guinhwyvare Robinhood - Maid Marian - B. Mordred -
Queen Agnes Alberts Dottir Crowned - D. Queen Matilda
Malcolmsdottir - B. Arthur Lord Wellington

May 2 - B. Catherine the Great

May 6 - Sacred Wells Day - Inghean Bhuidhe Day - Nerthus - Fons Lady of Fountains - Lady Melusina the Well Monster - Jette Priestess of Hertha Honoured - D. Eyvind Kelve - D. King Thrasamund

May 7 - Otto the Great Day - Ard Righ Made Known

May 8 - Furry Dance - D. Friedrich von Schiller

May 9 - D. Warrior Guthroth

May 11 - Eclipse - D. King Erkenbert

May 13 - Lemuralia -B. Empress Maria Theresa - Queen Jacqueline of Baveria Crowned

May 14 - Winds Day - Boreas - Skadi

May 15 - Mercuriala - Cold Sophie Mercury - Merlin Princess Melora - D. Valentinian - Blanch Lady Arundel Victory

May 16 - Manannans Day - Bran Voyage to Avalon - D. Princess Tudful Brychansdottir

May 19 - D. King Everth Oswysson - D. Anne Boleyn

May 20 - Mjolnir Day - Bendis the Huntress Day

May 21 - Agonium Vediovis - Anastesaria

May 22 - Hyankinthia Hyakinthos - Ajax Major Honoured - B. Wilhelm Richard Wagner

May 25 - D. King Edmund I of England

May 26 - D. Witch Alse Young

May 27 - Frigga Blot

May 28 - B. Thomas Moore

May 29 - Ambarvalia - Oak Apple Day - Yakbob - Ceres - Libera - Liber - Sylvanus - Bacchus - Venus Queen Kwyllog - King Charles II of England Honoured

May 30 - Moerae - Memorial Day - Camlann Day - Joan of Arc Fest - King Arthur Pendragon Passing - D. Mordred - D. Sir Lucan of Camelot D. Warrior Queen Tomyris - D. Odbrict King of Norway - D. Henry II King of England -D. Reginald II King of Mann - D. Christopher Marlowe - D. Sir Lemenic,

Ulrilda Priestess of Freyja - Lady Scenmed - Day for Morgan the Fay - Queen Northgalis - Queen Out Islands - Sir Bedevere

Jun 1 - Carnea Fest - Juno Moneta Fest - Tempestas Juno - Carnea - Hebe - Queen Antianara
Jun 2 - Ursula Mother Shipton Sontheil Honoured - Eurddil Pepiausdottir - Priestess of Mocca
Jun 5 - Sheela Na Gig
Jun 8 - Lindisfarne Day - D. King Hardecanute of England Jun 9 - Vestalia - Queen Frithogitha Honoured
Jun 13 - Pyanepsia - Skirophoria - Eponas Day, Lysippe - Peisinoe - Hippothoe – Harmothoe - Queen Reinmeth - Sir Aducht of Koln - Priestess Margaret Ningilbert - Richmodis Priestess of Epona Jun 14 - Vidars Day - Day for the Muses - Lady Ducaud Laborde Poncet Skill at Arms, Ligeia
Jun 17 - Turnipman Day
Jun 20 - D. Iron Skegge of Breida
Jun 21 - Aerra Litha - Alban Hefin - Heraeum Queen Aella - Admete - Priestess of Hera, D. John Skelton - D. Alban
Jun 22 - Sonnen Wende - Buphonia - Herculeum Artemis - Hercules - Helios – Omphale, Owen Glendower Victory at Bryn Glas
Jun 23 - Goursav Heol - Midsummer Eve - Apollo Hyperion - Helios - Queen Findmor - Lugus
Jun 24 - Caevron - Midsummer - Fors Fortuna – D. Dejanira - Hyperion - Helios - Apollo - Lugus Death of Balder
Jun 25 - Initium Aestatis - Arretophoria Goddess Aestas Day – Andromeda, D. Conan I of Britany
Jun 28 - D. Gerhard von Scharnhorst

Jul 4 - Independence Day - B. Nathaniel Hawthorne

Jul 5 - Feill Sheathain - Synoika - Bawming Day

Jul 6 - Julian the Blessed Birthday - Owen Roe O'Neil Ship
Landing - Rose O'Neil

Jul 7 - Caprotinae - Feriae Ancillarum - Juno - Jupiter - Minerva
D. Anna Hansen Priestess of Hades Jul 9 - Unn the Deep
Minded - Ketilsdottir - Amalasuntha Theodricsdottir -
D. Queen Arsinoe

Jul 10 - Heltag - Holdas Day - Lady Godiva's Ride - Knut the
Reaper Honoured - Lady Guro Rysserova Priestess of Hel -
Sidsel Mortensen - Priestess of Holda - Bodil Kvams Priestess
of Holda

Jul 11 - Panathenaea - Drostan Fest

Jul 15 - Antiope Day - Swithuns Day - Rowana Day Goddess
Rowana Princess Hrothwena - D. Matilda of Tuscany

Jul 17 - D. - Charlotte Corday

Jul 18 - D - Lady Thorgerd Holgabrud - D. John Dee D.
Godefroy de Bouillon Duke of War

Jul 23 – Neptunalia Rhein Maidens Woglinde. Weilgunde
Flosshilde Sunna - Sulis - Doris - Salacia – Neptune

Jul 25 - Furrinalia - Fal Stone Day - Crowning Day - Furrina -
Fand - King James I of England Crowning - King Dathi Struck
by Lightning - D. Samuel Taylor Coleridge

Jul 26 - Sleipnir Blot - Carl Bellman Fest

Jul 28 - Day for the Pythais Pythais Mother of Pythagoras -
Prophetess Manto - Delphi Priestess Phoebad - D. Magnus
Maximus

Jul 29 - Princess Cyrene and Her Lions Day - D. Sacrifice of
King Olaf Haraldsson

Aug 1 - Lughnassadh - Tailltenn Games - Puck Fair Dryads Day
- Cuiteach Fuait – Spring Lady Elyned - Lugh - Tailtiu - Aine
- Lady Eire - Carman Macha - Halfdan the High - Lady

Pherenice Niall Mac Eochaid - Cormac Mac Art - King
Roderick O'Conor - Queen Zarina - D. Queen Anne of
England

Aug 2 - Lammas Morrow Lamasthu - Atalanta - D. King
William Rufus of England

Aug 3 - D. King Henry III of France

Aug 5 - D. King Oswald of Northumbria King Penda Victory

Aug 6 - D. King Griffin Ap Cynan B. Alfred Baron Tennyson

Aug 9 - King Radbrod Day Emperor - Valens Slain

Aug 12 - D. Offa Ap Thingferth - D. William Blake

Aug 13 - Nemoralia - Diana Assembly - Sapho Fest - King
Numa - Dedication of Spring - Harrow Rite Celebration of
Nymphs of Springs - Warrior Poetess Telesilla Cross Dress
Fest, Egeria Lady Advisor to King Numa - Nemesis Honoured

Aug 14 - D. Duncan I King of Scotland

Aug 15 - D. Queen Philippa of Hainaut

Aug 16 - Minstrals Day - Lady Oddibjord - Sanant Queen of
Gwenedd - Tristvardd - Bard Lady Chysothenius, Walther
von der Vogelweide - Mainferdic Bard Lady Nausicaa - Bard
Lady Lavercam - Llywarch -Hen - Avan Verddig – Eliot -
Aneurin

Aug 19 - Vinalia Rustica - Venus - Jupiter - Pan - Bacchus -
Sylvanus - Helen of Troy - Lady Hiera

Aug 20 - Zakynthos - Semele Rites, Celebration of Death of
Bacchus - Hades - Queen Minthe - Priestess Autonoe -
Priestess Ino - Priestess Agave - Lady Macris - Lady Evoe

Aug 23 - Vulcanalia - Vertumnalia - Nemesia Lady Aedesia -
D. William Wallace

Aug 24 - Mania - Queen Umbraefel Maurice Dottir

Aug 25 - Rune Day - Opiconsiva - King Cole Fest, Lord
Mauries Day - Wotan Ordeal - Ops - Consus - Spes - Ceres
- D. Emperor Gratian - D. Henry Morgan, D. Queen Margaret

of Anjou

Aug 28 - Frey Faxi Blot - Red Aoife Wed Richard Strongbow - B. Johann Wolfgang Von Goethe

Aug 29 - Urdatag - D. Augustus Caesar

Aug 30 - D. Theodoric the Great - D. Witch Agnes Waterhouse

Sep 3 - D. Maelsechiann II - D. Garret Fitzgerald

Sep 5 - Pipers Day - Horn Dance - Pan - Cornely - D. Emperor Eugenius - D. King Arbogast

Sep 6 - Labour Day - King Herman Fest -King Herman of Teutonberg - Perkin Warbeck

Sep 9 - Asclepigenias Day - D. Fransez II Duke of War - D. King Herman

Sep 10 - D. Matilda Augusta Empress Maud

Sep 12 - Harvest Home - Kernfest - Demetria

Sep 13 - Lectisternia - Cornely Fest - Craft Fair - Corndoll Honoured - Jupiter - Juno - Minerva - Proserpine - Ceres

Sep 14 - B. Heinrich Cornelius Agrippa

Sep 17 - Hildegarde von Bingen Day - D. Walter Savage Landor

Sep 20 - B. Alexander the Great - D. King Elwald of Northumbria - Bright Spot Seen Where King Elwald Died - Queen Thalestris Honoured

Sep 21 - D. Raud the Strong - Sighvat Lawspeaker Sep 22 - Vidarfest - D. Vergilius Publius Maro

Sep 23 - Julia Drusilla Named High Priestess - B. Euripides

Sep 24 - Elved Erntedank - Eleusinia - Forsette Day - Albrecht von Wallenstein Day - Europa - King Minos - King Rhadamanthus - Astraea - Syn - Goll Mac Morna - Ariadne - Queen Marcia Proba - B. Paracelsus

Sep 25 - D. Priestess Emerenziana Pichler

Sep 26 - Thesmorphia - B. Johnny Appleseed Chapman

Sep 28 - Ziza Fest - Seigfriedblot - Brunhild Tag - Gwyn Ap Nudd Wild Hunt - Gudruns Ride

Sep 29 - Braderie - Wenceslaus Fest - Carrot Fest - Bridget - B. Horatio Lord Nelson

Oct 1 - Tigillum Soroium - Fides Day
Oct 7 - D. Edgar Allan Poe
Oct 8 - Burgomistress Kenau Hasselaer Victory
Oct 9 - Filicitas Fest - Leif Eiriksson Landing - D. Witch Catherine Peyretonne - Lady Freydis
Oct 14 - Cadixtus Day - Vinternat - Battle of Hastings - D. King Harold II of England - D. Minstral Taillefer - William the Conqueror Victory
Oct 17 - Hengest Fest - Lord Wittenmoot Honoured
Oct 18 - Hernefest - Priestess Pandrosos Day
Oct 19 - Armilustrum - Queen Radigund Fest
Oct 21 - Koureotis - Ursula Day - End of Battle Trafalgar Day - Bravalla Battle - D. Horatio Lord Nelson - D. Lady Webiorg - D. Standard - Bearer Lady Heid - D. Lady Wisna - D. Hethna Queen of Zealand - Juliana of Pacy - D. King Harald Wartooth Hilditonn - King Sigurth Ring - Emma of Norfolk
Oct 26 - D. Athelstan King of England - Emilja Plater Ksawerysdottir
Oct 28 - Fyribod Fest - Ngetal Day - D. Queen Margaret Valdemarsdottir - D. Lord Rigwatle
Oct 29 - B. John Keats
Oct 31 - Halloween - D. Crimhthann Cass King of Connacht - Witch Queen Onbrawst - Witch Biddy Early - Warrior Witch Harthgrepa

Nov 1 - Samhain – Apaturia Skuld - Spes - D. Edmund Ironside - D. Diarmaid Mac Cerbail - D. Muirchthach Mac Erca - D. Lord Ethelnoth - D. Conaire Mor Mac Nessa - Rose Hallybread
Nov 3 - King Hubert's Day -D. King Clydawg

Nov 8 - Godefroy's Day - D. Witch Bessy Dunlop

Nov 9 - Sigrid Queen of Sweden - Empress Helena

Nov 10 - Einherjar Eve - Hollantide - Wild Hunt - Ride of
Nincnevin Dark Daughter of Bones - Skogul the Valkyrie -
Starkad the Old - Green Lady Godda - Dietrich Von Bern -
Eckhardt Gatekeeper of Hurselberg - Lady Genofeva Von
Andernach - Hans Trapp - Sir Rupprecht - Sir Amelung -
Wild Edric - Valkyrie Guth -Valkyrie Thruth

Nov 11 - Schudderkorf - Hero Day - Blackthorn Fest -
Lunantishees Day - Gaensetag - Selene Rites - Queen
Cartimandua - Queen Melanippe - Queen Olga of Russia -
Princess Aefa - Thornbjorg Queen of Sweden - Sir Kay -
Thyra Queen of Denmark - Sir Tristram - Freydis Eiriksdottir
- Princess Rusilla - Warrior Maiden Pantariste - Hector -
Princess Aethelflaed Alfredsdottir - Queen Myrine - Etzel the
Hun - Lady Hrist - Queen Orithia - Queen Minythia - Lady
Euryale - Iliach MacRury - Lady Thoe - Lady Thermodosa -
Princess Sichelgaita - Lady Prothoe - Lady Tecmessa - Lady
Rorei - Lady Mederei Badellfawr - Lady Thraso - Warrior
Woman Flora MacDonald - Lady Scyleia - Lady Sarka -
Lady Stickla - Lady Kydoime - Lady Randgrith - Lady Florine
- Lady Ainippe - Lady Bremusa - Lady Giesela of Eltz -
Lady Pyrgomache - Warrior Woman Marie Schellinck -Lady
Iphito - Lady Herfjioturr - Lady Glauke - Lady Skeggjoild -
Queen Messene - Warrior Woman Thusnelda - Lady
Geiravor - Lady Reginleif -Lady Teisipyle - Lady Clonie -
LLewei Seitwedsdottir - Lady Mimnousa - Lady Augusta
Kruger - Princess Arachidamia - Lady Turfida - Princess
Camilla - Lady Alkaia - Lady Andromache - Lady Evandre -
Warrior Woman Hannah Witneg - Lady Eumache - Lady
Derinoe -Lord Hingwar - D. Canute the Great

Nov 13 - Feronia - D. Gerald Fitzgerald

Nov 14 - Mocca Fest - Dubric Day - Lady Alcippe Honoured

Nov 16 - Hecatenacht - D. Edmund King of Eastanglia -
D. Margaret Queen of Scots Edwardsdottir - Sagana Priestess
of Hecate

Nov 17 - Volkstravertag - Gertrude the Great

Nov 20 - Priestess Praetextatus - Priestess Paulina

Nov 21 - D. Henry Purcell

Nov 22 - Ydalir - Spirit World Music Fest - Ull - Bridget -
Terpsichore - Amergin - Bragi -Polymnia - Bard Dygunnelw
- Bard Tuan MacCairill - D. Robinhood

Nov 23 - Thanksgiving - Welandfest - Clement First the
Advocate of Smiths

Nov 25 - Arianrhods Day - Telchtereia - Gaia Fest - White Ship
Sinking Remembrance

Nov 28 - Sophia Day - Queen Dejanira Honoured

Dec 1 - Banshees Day - Pythagoras Death Ritual - D. Henry I
King of England

Dec 5 - Nicks Eve - Poseidea - Faunus Eve

Dec 6 - Nicktag - Panfest - King Natanleod

Dec 7 - Haloia - Kormak Ogmundarsson the Bard

Dec 8 - Queen Christina of Sweden - B. Mary Queen of Scots

Dec 9 - Egil Skalla Grimssons Day

Dec 10 - D. King Llywelyn the Last

Dec 11 - Bruma's Day

Dec 12 - D. Warrior Woman Phoebe Hessel

Dec 13 - Lucia Day - Lucina Day

Dec 15 - D. King Ottocar I

Dec 16 - D. Priestess Alison Balfour - B. Ludwig van Beethoven

Dec 18 – Epona Fest

Dec 19 - Opalia - Tullus Hostilius

Dec 21 - Angeronalia - Arthran - Divalia - King Arthur

Pendragon

Dec 22 - B. Pryderi

Dec 23 - Saturnalia - Larentalia - Unhewn Stone Day - Stone Witch Long Meg Honoured

Dec 24 - Nodlaig Eve - Heiligabend - Christmas Eve - Weihnachtsgrusse - Modraniht - Nick - Sylvanus - Hertha - Ullanissen - Vesta

Dec 25 - Yule - Christmas

Dec 26 - Boxing - Ranfest - Frey Return - D. Lady Killigrew

Dec 27 - Ash Day - B. Johannes Kepler

Dec 29 - D. Thomas a Becket Sacrifice

Dec 31 - Hogmanay - Ogmagogs Day - Crow Goddess Natosuelta

DARK WATER AND NIGHT

Darkness of night   Dark still water
Angels of dark water and night
Silently   float past —
Away to the left   out on the water
A gold hair bent out then in
A bent thread on the water —
In the darkness   over the water
Pale white   three angels pass
Strike the gold hair nerve
Khaaaaaaaaaa
   Kaaaaaaaaaaaa
They scream
Two   then the center angel   scream
Over the dark water   three angels pass
To the gold hair nerve
Khaaaaaaaaaa
   Kaaaaaaaaaaaa
They scream
Three pale angels   over the dark water
Pass   strike the gold hair nerve
Khaaaaaaaaaa
   Kaaaaaaaaaaaa
They scream
Ever coming Ever empty hollow singing
Ever singing Ever singing Ever singing
They scream They are gone
The singing scream   sings on

125

www.ingramcontent.com/pod-product-compliance
Lightning Source LLC
LaVergne TN
LVHW041226080426
835508LV00011B/1099